# A Lesson Learned

## It's Okay to be Different

## A Children's Book
### by
## Aaron Miller

*I want to thank my husband Shaun for always being supportive in my choices in life and the encouragement he gives to me in achieving my dreams. I want to express the love and gratitude that I have for our children, Ashton and Kensly, who inspired me to move forward and publish this book that I wrote when I was 14 years old. The message I was conveying in this book was not only important then, but it is also still an important message in today's world. Shaun, Ashton, and Kensly, I love you with all my heart and soul.*

Albert was a very sad little raccoon. There wasn't a day that passed when all the other raccoons would make fun of him. But why did the other raccoons make fun of poor Albert? You see, Albert is an albino raccoon, which means that he is all white in color.

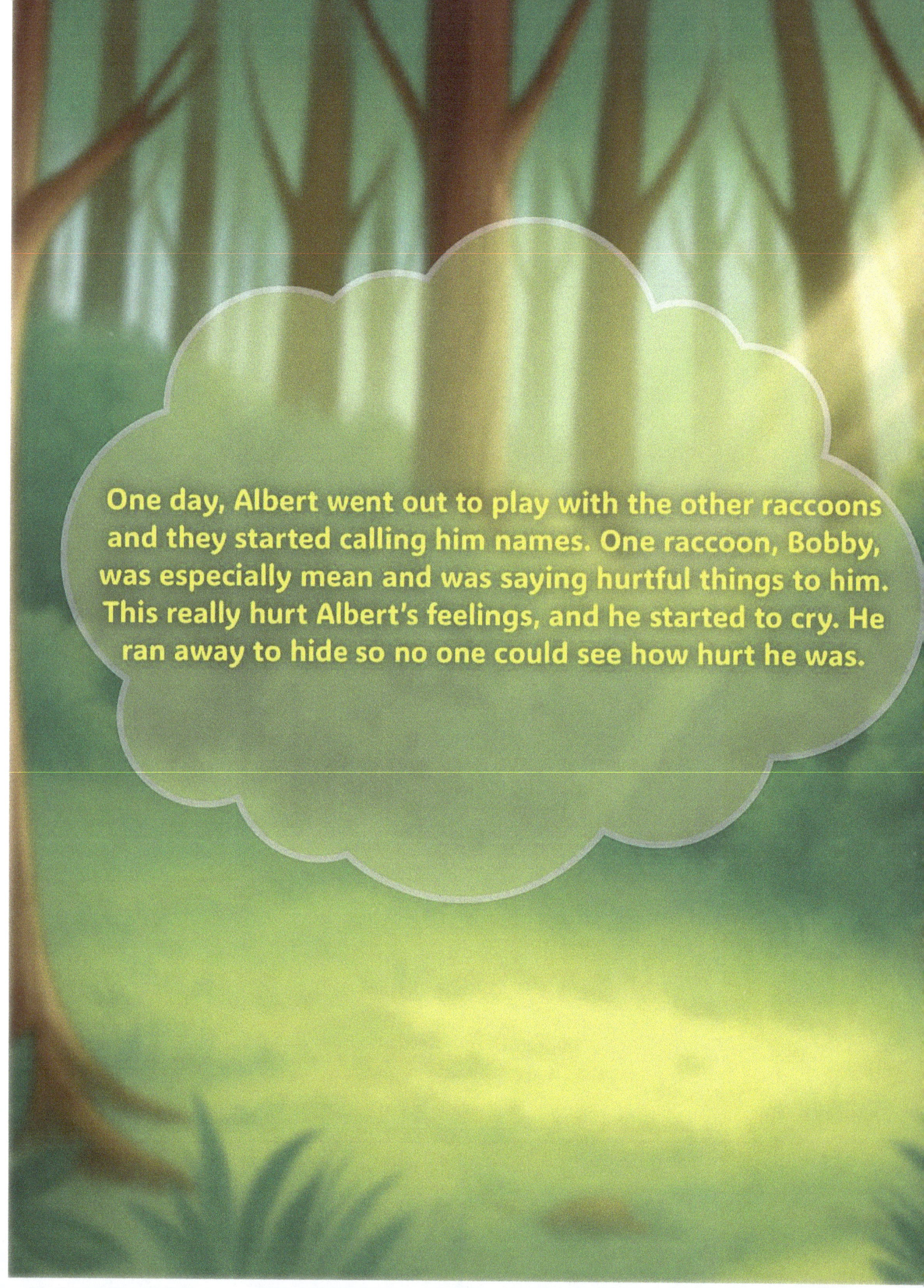

One day, Albert went out to play with the other raccoons and they started calling him names. One raccoon, Bobby, was especially mean and was saying hurtful things to him. This really hurt Albert's feelings, and he started to cry. He ran away to hide so no one could see how hurt he was.

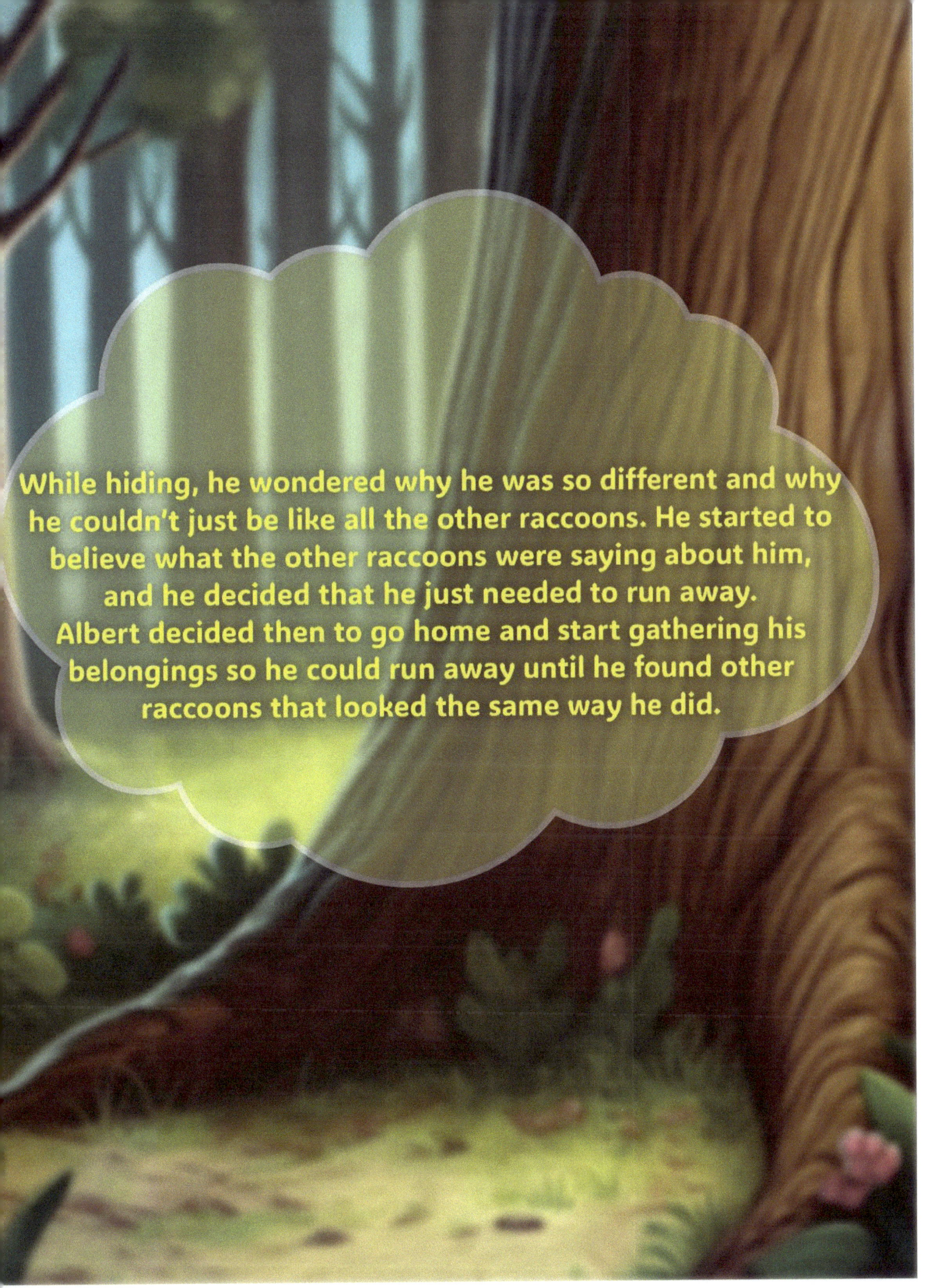

While hiding, he wondered why he was so different and why he couldn't just be like all the other raccoons. He started to believe what the other raccoons were saying about him, and he decided that he just needed to run away. Albert decided then to go home and start gathering his belongings so he could run away until he found other raccoons that looked the same way he did.

While Albert was packing his belongings, his younger sister Luna came in and Albert told her he was running away. Luna begged him not to and told him how much he was loved and how much would be missed.

Albert didn't believe it, for he had started to believe all the bad things that the other raccoons were saying about him. So, after gathering his belongings, he went off on his own in search of raccoons that looked like him, hoping that they would be more accepting than the ones he grew up with.

After leaving his forest that he called home, he came upon another forest patch and had big hopes that there would be raccoons here that looked like him so he would fit in. After searching and searching, he found no other raccoons that looked like him and the ones he met said hurtful things to him like the other raccoons in his home forest. Hurt by this, Albert continued through on his journey.

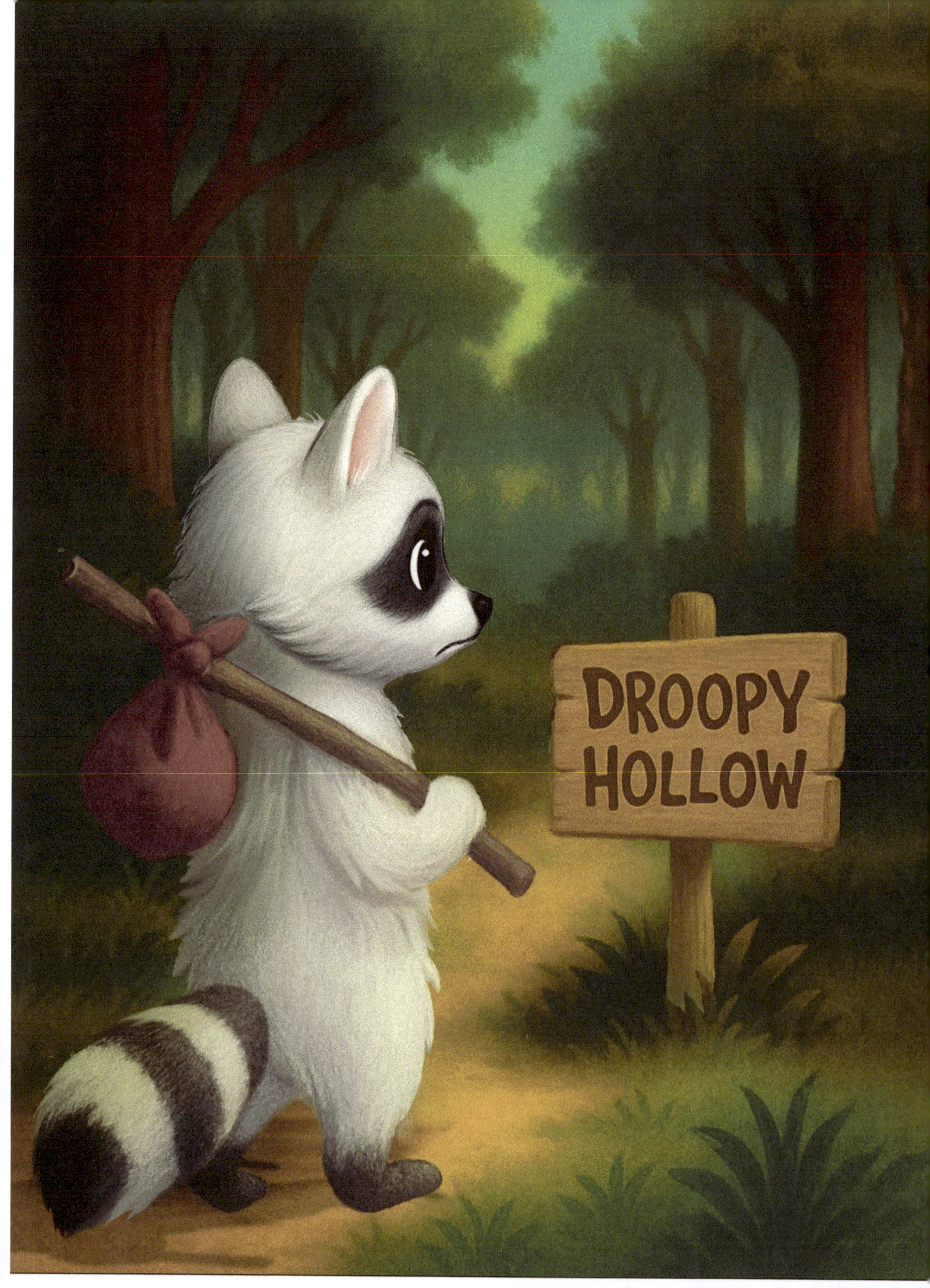
DROOPY
HOLLOW

Albert's next stop was at the forest of Droopy Hollow. This was a much larger forest than his home, and he was very hopeful that he would find raccoons that looked just like him!

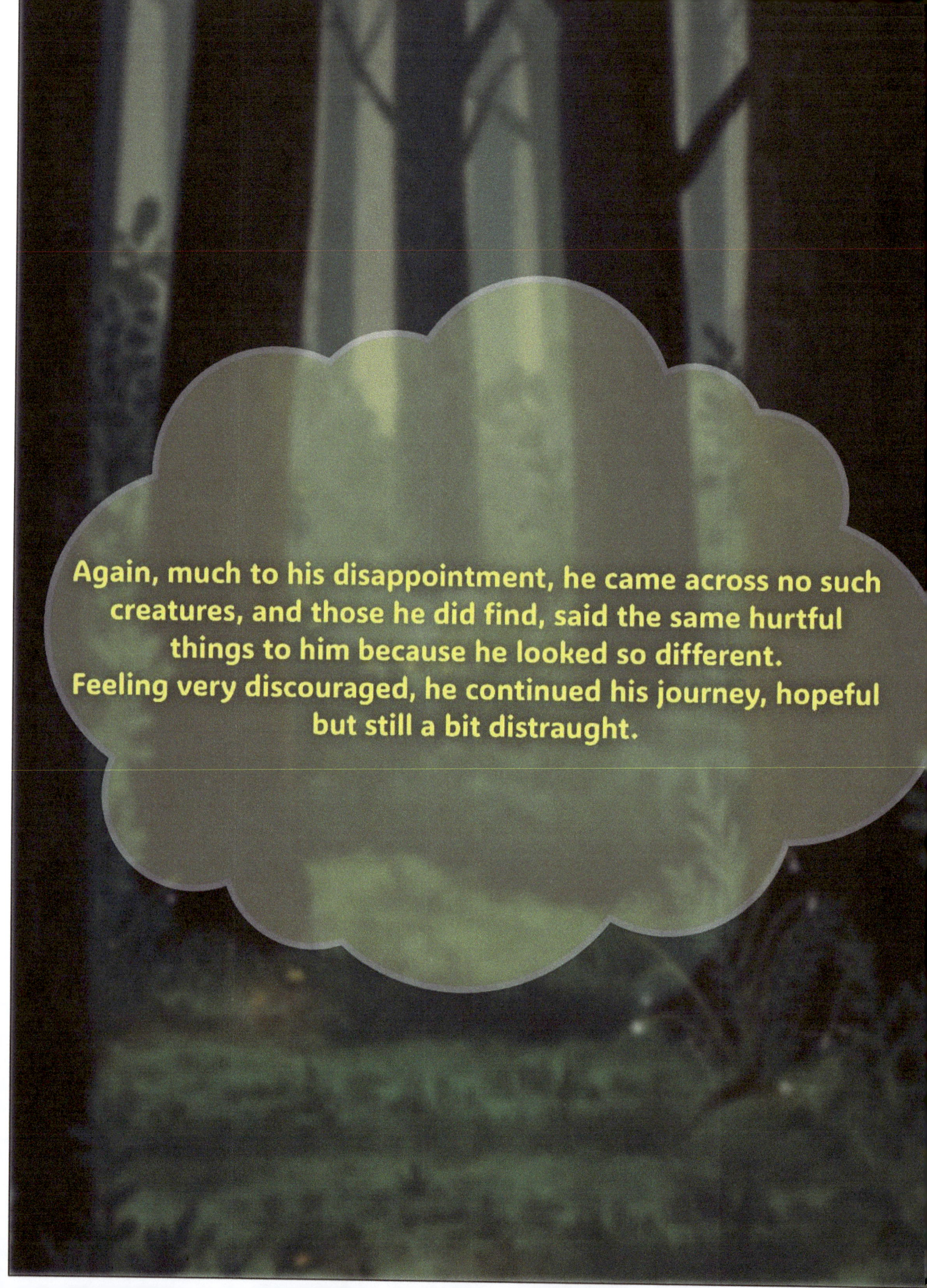

Again, much to his disappointment, he came across no such creatures, and those he did find, said the same hurtful things to him because he looked so different.
Feeling very discouraged, he continued his journey, hopeful but still a bit distraught.

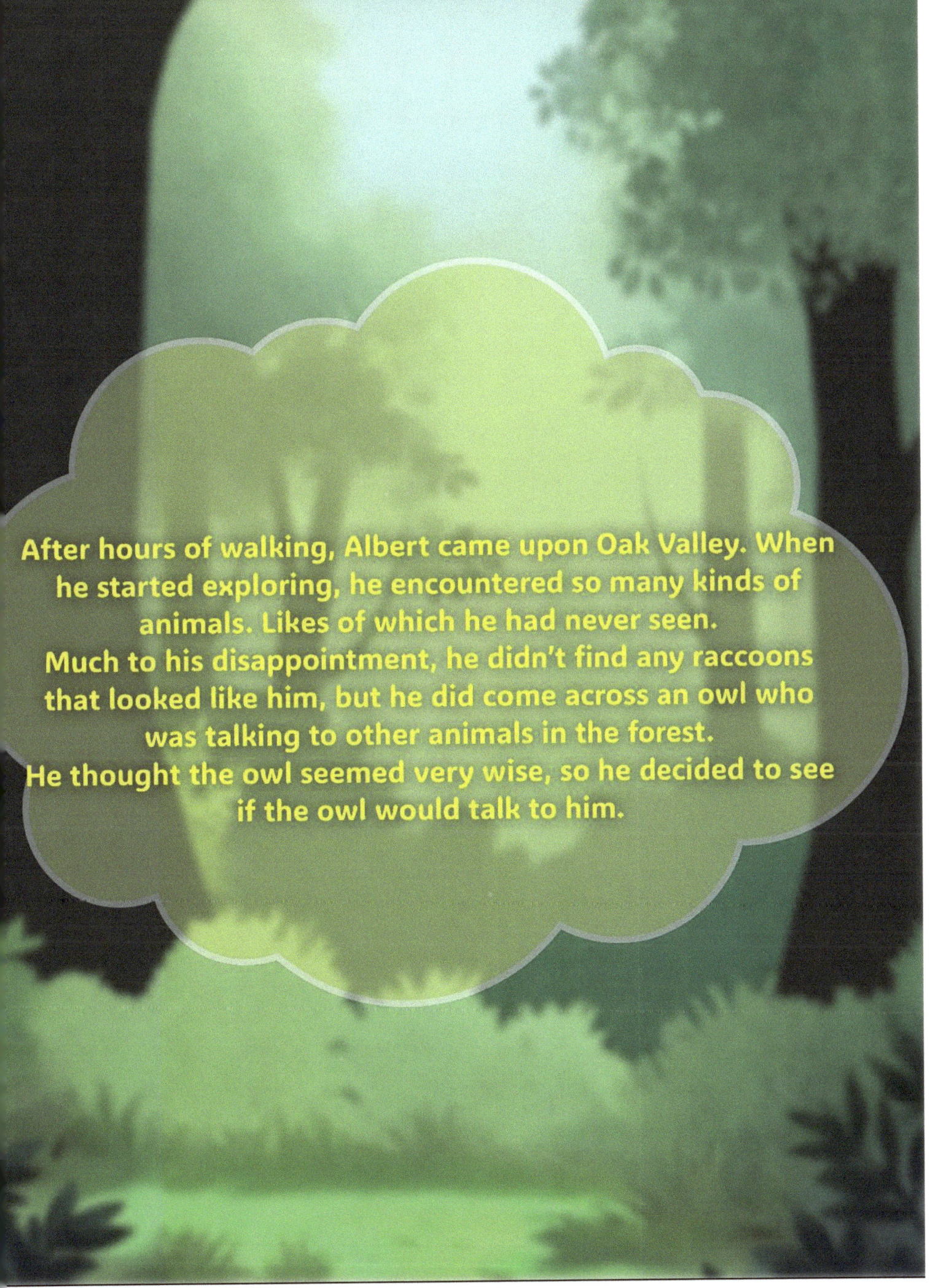

After hours of walking, Albert came upon Oak Valley. When he started exploring, he encountered so many kinds of animals. Likes of which he had never seen.

Much to his disappointment, he didn't find any raccoons that looked like him, but he did come across an owl who was talking to other animals in the forest.

He thought the owl seemed very wise, so he decided to see if the owl would talk to him.

Albert went up to the group of animals and the owl. When the owl spotted Albert approaching, the owl said, "Well look here, it's not often we get to see the likes of this!"
Albert thought to himself that this was another animal that was just going to start making fun of him just because he was different and started to become upset.
Albert asked the wise owl, "Why do you want to make fun of me? Why am I so different?"

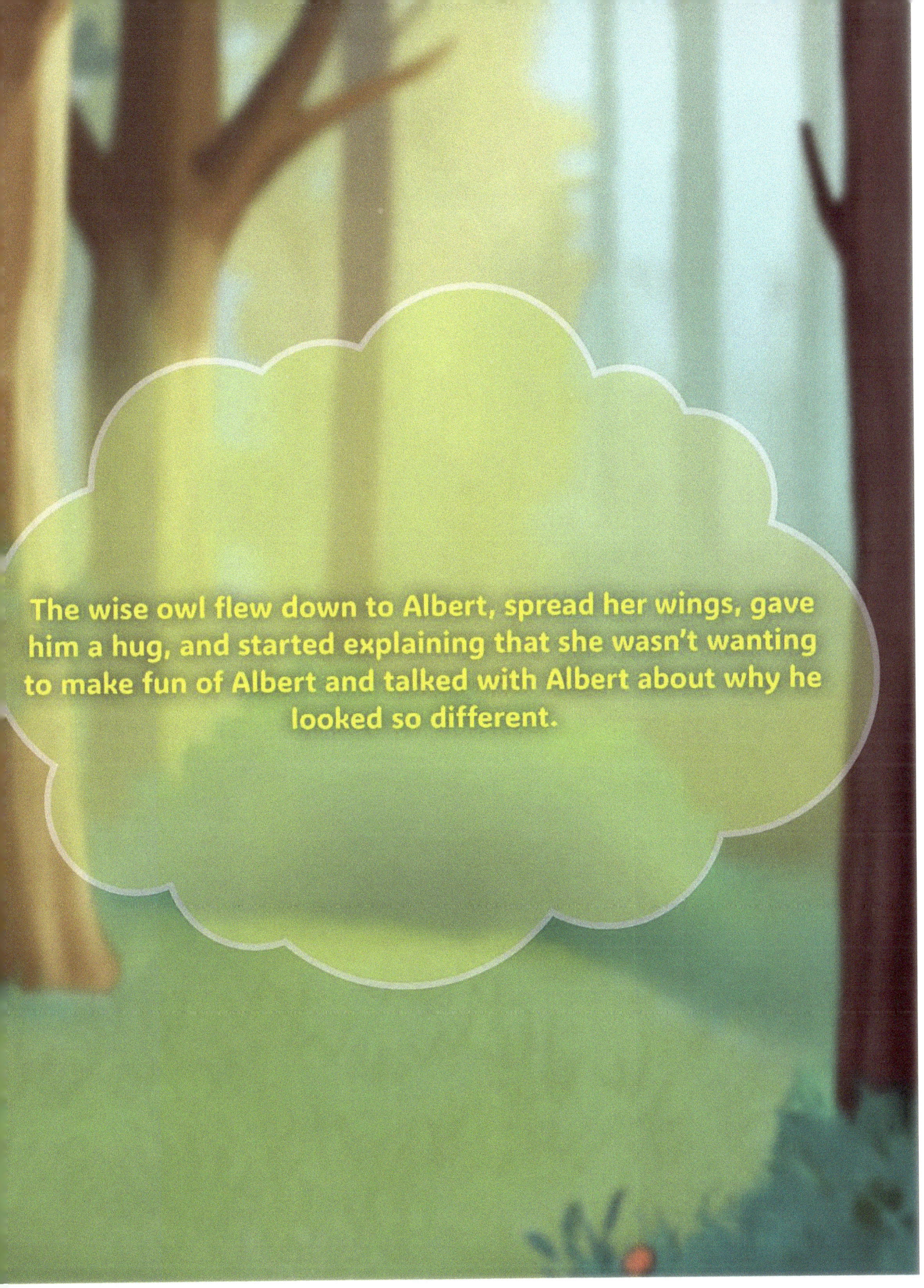

The wise owl flew down to Albert, spread her wings, gave him a hug, and started explaining that she wasn't wanting to make fun of Albert and talked with Albert about why he looked so different.

The owl smiled and said, "Albert, you are rare—not wrong. Just like the moon glows differently from the sun, you shine in your own special way. Being different doesn't make you less, it makes you, you."

For the first time, Albert didn't feel ashamed. He felt... proud.

After hearing what the wise owl had to say, Albert became so happy and filled with joy. He had his hope back! He thanked the wise owl, gave her a hug in return, and then decided he wanted to return home to share what he had learned with his family and friends.

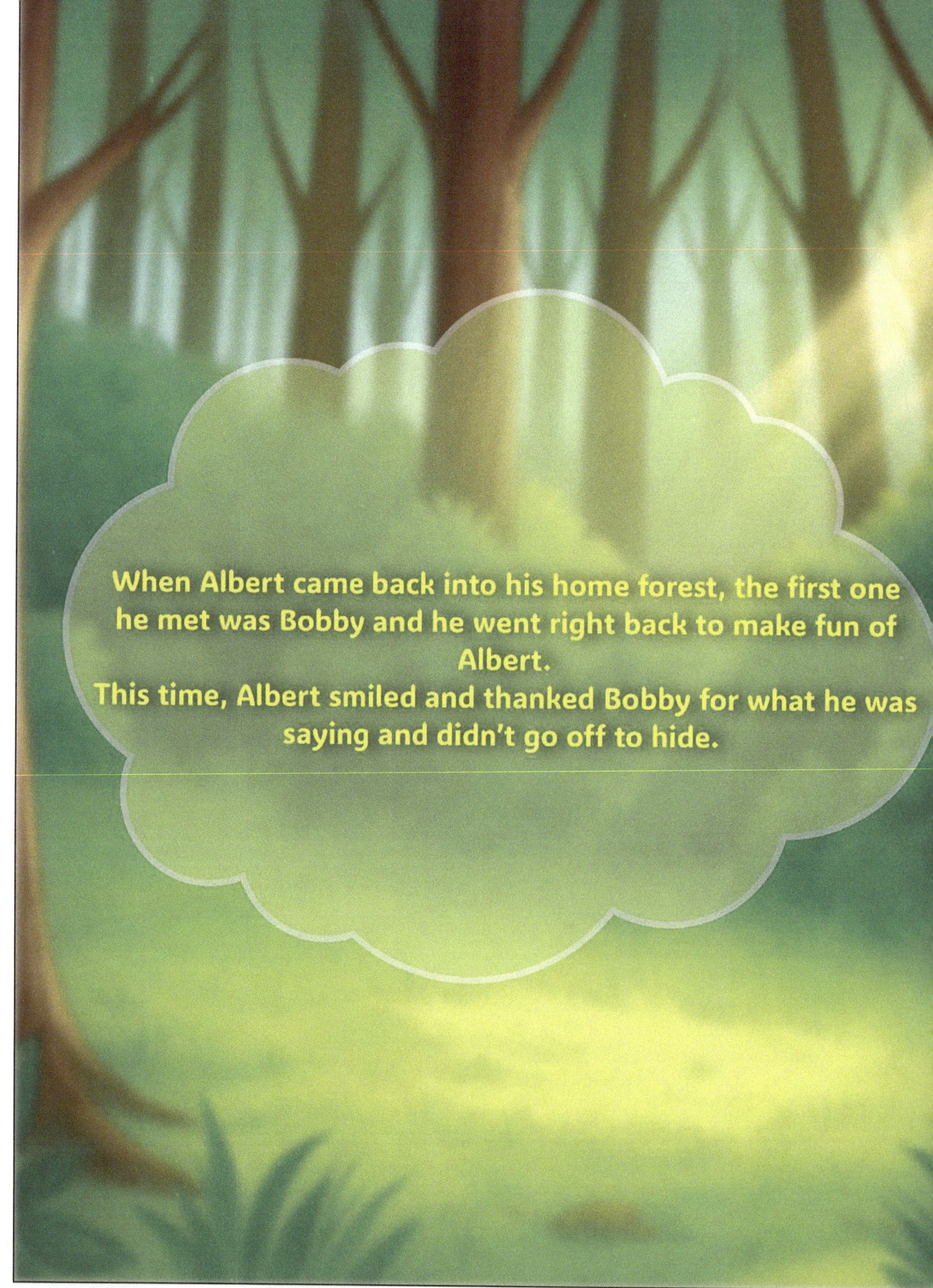

When Albert came back into his home forest, the first one he met was Bobby and he went right back to make fun of Albert.
This time, Albert smiled and thanked Bobby for what he was saying and didn't go off to hide.

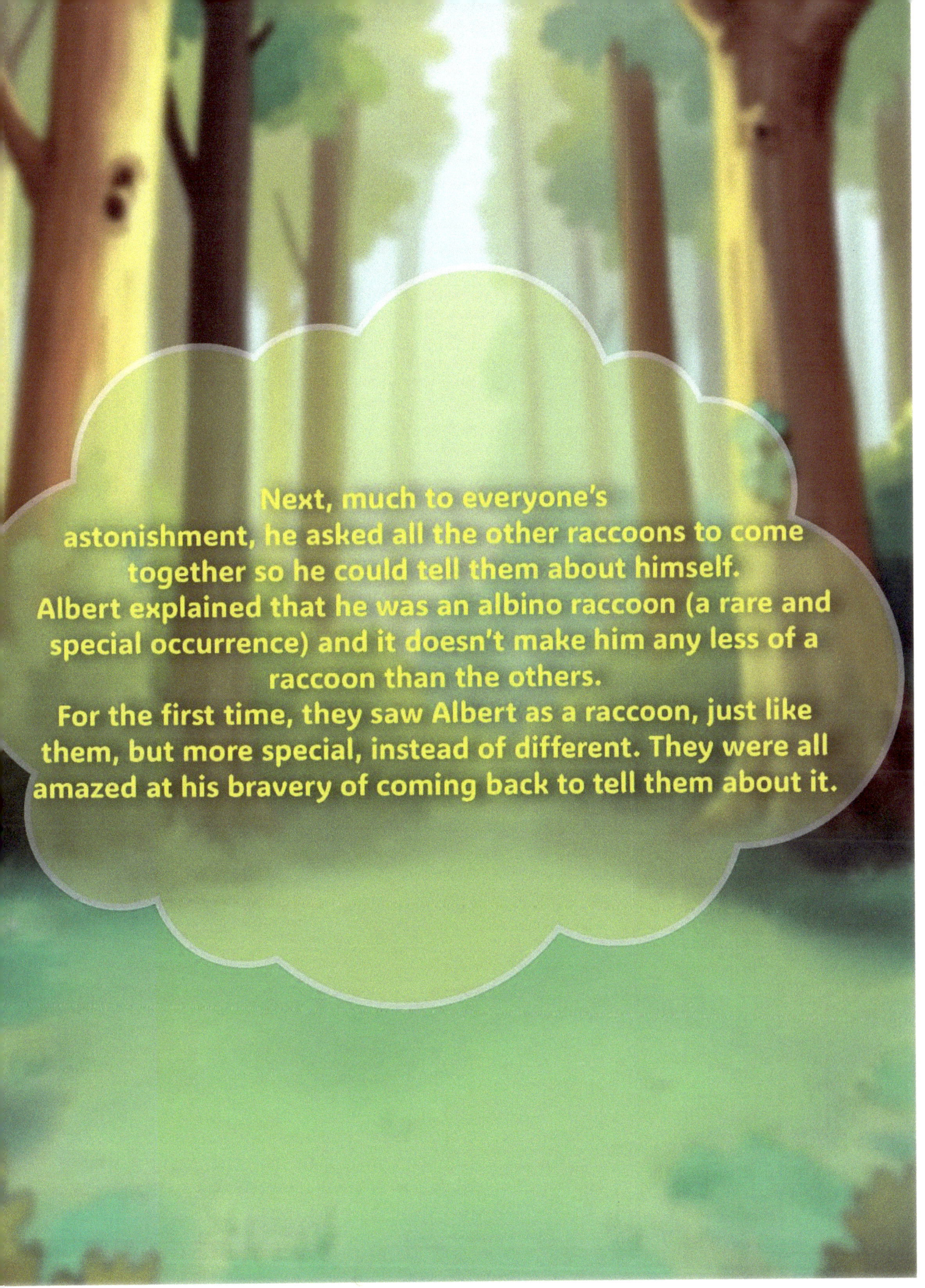

Next, much to everyone's astonishment, he asked all the other raccoons to come together so he could tell them about himself.
Albert explained that he was an albino raccoon (a rare and special occurrence) and it doesn't make him any less of a raccoon than the others.
For the first time, they saw Albert as a raccoon, just like them, but more special, instead of different. They were all amazed at his bravery of coming back to tell them about it.

Bobby was the first one to approach Albert and apologized
for the hurtful things he had been saying to him.
Then, Bobby, along with all the other raccoons in the forest,
one by one promised to never make fun of any other animal
for any reason.
They came to realize that saying hurtful things can really
hurt others, and that it is also better to learn about
differences instead of thinking everyone needs to look and
be the same.

# WHICH LESSON WILL ALBERT

# LEARN NEXT?